Overcomers in Jesus Christ

A Testimonial, Praise and Worship Book

Arletta Lockett

Scripture quotations marked KJV are from the Holy Bible,
King James Version (Authorized Version). First published
in 1611. Quoted from the KJV Classic Reference Bible,
Copyright © 1983 by The Zondervan Corporation.

To order additional copies of this book, contact:
Xlibris
844-714-8691
www.Xlibris.com
Orders@Xlibris.com

ISBN: Softcover   978-1-6641-2534-6
       EBook   978-1-6641-2535-3

Print information available on the last page

Rev. date: 09/14/2020

Overcomers
in
Jesus Christ

Introduction

This book of different beautiful testimonies and praises was given to share how God has delivered each of them in many situations in their lives.

In my praise and worship time with God, I was over-whelmed by the spirit of God, thanking and praising Him for all His blessings to me and my family. I felt lead by the Holy Spirit to ask others to join me and share their testimony and praises in a book for others to read and be uplifted and encouraged. God wants his people to never forget what he has done for each of us in our lives.

These are testimonies of the saints of God and others who love Him also.

"Let every thing that hath breath praise the Lord, Praise ye the Lord" (Psalm 150:6 KJV).

Dedication

In reading this book, you will be a part of the journeys of God's people. In each testimony, you will fill a part of their struggles, sufferings, and victories.

To all who contributed by sharing their awesome testimonies and praises to the glory of God. You are truly overcomers in Jesus Christ.

"And they overcame him by the blood of the lamb, and by the word of their testimony; and they loved not their lives unto the death" (Revelation 12:11 KJV).

Acknowledgments

With special thanks to God almighty. I thank and praise you every day from the bottom of my soul for blessing me in every way to do this testimonial and praise book, and for giving me the mind, the ability, and the strength to finish this wonderful project. My purpose is to share with the world your love and goodness.

To all the *participants* who so gratefully shared their testimonies and praises of God's blessings in their lives, I say, *Thank you.*

To my loving husband Jeremiah Lockett Sr., Thank you for your awesome love and support. I love you dearly.

Contents

The Lord's Prayer

"After this manner therefore pray Ye: Our Father which art in heaven, Hallowed be thy name. Thy Kingdom come. Thy will be done in earth, as it is in heaven. Give us this day our daily bread. And forgive us our debts, as we forgive our debtors. And lead us not into temptation, but deliver us from evil: For thine is the Kingdom, and the power, and the glory, for ever. Amen" (Matthew 6:9–13).

O Give Thanks

In October 2014, I found a lump on my left breast. In November, I received an appointment for a mammogram. During this visit, something was found in both breasts. I could tell that the nurses were concerned about my peacefulness. My prayer was to put this in the Lord's hands.

As I was returning back to the Pentecostal Assemblies of the World (PAW) headquarter, I called my husband, my son, and daughter to share my results. They were set back but know that we can only trust the Lord and my faith journey was starting. But I had no fear and knows the Lord makes no mistakes.

I thank God for this faith journey and those who went with me: my family, friends, spiritual mothers, prayer warriors, Bishop Lambert W. Gates Sr., Bishop Charles H. Ellis III, Bishop Michael D. Hannah Sr., the cancer survivors, the medical team, and the PAW headquarter staff and many, many others.

December was a month of many happenings: cancer treatment plans—six months chemotherapy with four aggressive treatments and six–seven weeks of daily radiation treatments; the insert of a port, a catheter (port) in my chest; surgery to remove two cancers one from each breast and seven lump nodes (some had cancer cells). A few days later, I had my first treatment. I received a blood clot located in my jugular vein that never moved. If it had moved, the result would have been death. I was surely thankful.

God had the clot remain in the same place until it was dissolved by blood thinner injections. I administered it in my abdomen every twelve hours for months. The first port was removed, but another one was inserted on the opposite side of my chest, and the result was no complications. But Jesus makes no mistakes.

In my journey, I had side effects from chemo and radiation treatments: low blood count, discolored and damaged nails, medical bruising, two admissions to the hospital for blood transfusions, lack of energy and fatigue, numbness in both feet and both hands, radiation burns, and yes, complete hair loss. I continued to have side effects in 2016 and even now. Through all of my chemotherapy, God never permitted any vomiting or any nausea. I find *no* fault in him.

If the Lord was not on my side, I do not know where I will be. I thank God for my children's strong support and their love. I also thank God for my husband. He has been a pillar of strength each and every day. He provided whatever my needs were and are, as well as his unconditional love. Oh, my medical team was given to me. God gave them knowledge for and about me. With many we have become family and friends today.

God gave me the determination and strength to have His faith during these treatments. I worked throughout this journey unless I had medical appointments. I thank God for this journey in life, his love, and a mind of no fear. I believe God permitted this journey, so I could give him all the praise. I thank him for all the valleys and the mountain tops, mostly the valleys. But most of all, for helping others who may come this way.

I know he did it for me; he can do it for you.

Jesus is faithful.

Testimony of Carolyn A. Darring, Indianapolis, Indiana

Because Jesus Loves Me

Do you recall the old Sunday school song, "Jesus Loves Me?" This song helped me survive heartbreak at a young age. I became a ward of the state as a child. During that time, I attended therapy to assist me in coping with the abuse and rejection I experienced. During one of the sessions, the therapist read the predicted outcome of my life.

It read as such, "I wouldn't graduate high school. I wouldn't get married. I'd have children by multiple men. I wouldn't retain custody of my children. I'd be a drug user and abuser. I'd be an alcoholic." The list continued with more negative outcomes. My response was, "No! This is not my future!" The therapist asked me, "Why not?" My response was, "Because Jesus loves me! God did not birth me for that."

Those words have stuck with me since the day they were spoken. Thanks be to God; they have helped me focus on what God says about me instead of what man says about me.

"I will praise thee; for I am fearfully and wonderfully made: marvelous are thy works; and that my soul knoweth right well" (Ps. 139:14 KJV).

"For God so loved the world, that he gave his only begotten Son, that whosoever believeth in him should not perish, but have everlasting life" (John 3:16 KJV).

"For if ye forgive men their trespasses, your heavenly Father will also forgive you:" (Matt. 6:14 KJV).

"In all thy ways acknowledge him, and he shall direct thy paths" (Prov. 3:6 KJV).

"Beloved, I wish above all things that thou mayest prosper and be in health, even as thy soul prospereth" (3 John 1:2 KJV).

"The stone which the builders refused is become the head stone of the corner" (Ps. 118:22 KJV).

Being a statistic is a common excuse for people not to do the hard work to heal. Sometimes, it is easier to accept what is acceptable by others, then to stand alone in a dark place and hope for guidance and light. By the guidance of God, I have been blessed to do the following: I graduated high school on time. I married my high school sweetheart. We were blessed with two healthy children. Neither one of us are substance abusers. We both are educated at the master's degree level. I continue to believe *Jesus loves me* no matter what I experience in life.

"I can do all things through Christ which strengtheneth me" (Phil. 4:13 KJV).

Testimony of Audra Hagan, Leander, Texas

Joy

"Blessed is the people that know the joyful sound: They shall walk, O Lord, in the light of thy Countenance. In thy name shall they rejoice all the day: And in thy righteousness shall they be exalted" (Psalm 89:15-16 KJV).

Fruitfulness

"I am the true vine, and my Father is the husbandman. Every branch in me that beareth not fruit he taketh away: and every branch that beareth fruit, he purgeth it, that it may bring forth more fruit. Now ye are clean through the word which I have spoken unto you. Abide in me, and I in you. As the branch cannot bear fruit of itself, except it abide in the vine; no more can ye, except ye abide in me. I am the vine, ye are the branches: He that abideth in me, and I in him, the same bringeth forth much fruit: for without me ye can do nothing" (John 15:1-5 KJV).

To God Be the Glory

To God be all the glory. My testimony is how God protected us in our house when gas was escaping from inside. I don't know how long that had been going on. If my son-in-law had not been looking for cable boxes, we would not have known that the gas was leaking. He went into the basement to look for cable boxes, and that's when he discovered the odor of gas. It was extraordinarily strong. He thought it was coming from the hot water tank, but it was worse than that. It was coming from the pipes. We called the gas company, and they came out right away and shut the gas off. It was very cold; we were without heat and hot water.

God was so good to us. No one got sick. They had to put new pipes in. It took about five to six days. Our house could have had exploded. God kept his hand of protection and spared our lives.

Testimony of Elizabeth Walls, Gary, Indiana

I Will Never Forget

I will never forget when the Lord spoke a word into my life that changed me forever. We were at a general conference at Anaheim, California, on October 1984, sitting in the nose-bleed section during a worship service. The Lord spoke very clearly to me and instructed me that, when I returned home, I would be getting orders. I was leaving Altus, Oklahoma. It struck me with such a force that I sat down to gather myself to continue with the worship service.

Upon returning home, I received a call from my supervisor: "Oh, by the way, Ernie, you have orders. You're leaving." I asked, "Where?" and he said, "Guam." There is a lot that led up to my new appointment from the Lord. He had prepared me for my calling before the call to my work in his kingdom.

This began about an eleven-year journey in the foreign mission field I had an interest in, sparked by the testimony of the missionary, John Wolfram, about Asia. When we left Altus, the church was in the middle of a building program I was very much involved in, I did not want to leave, but the Lord knew how to handle that issue. So in February 1985, we arrived on the island of Guam, contacted the missionaries that attended a Wednesday night service, and showed up for the first workday on the church's newly purchased property on Saturday. It ended eleven years later with life-long friendships with many wonderful people. I have to mention two who were sent by God to my life, Brother and Sister Bettis, missionaries to Micronesia.

Testimony of Ernest Walls Jr., Navarre, Florida

What the Bible Is

1. The Bible is God's inspired revelation of the origin and destiny of all things. Here, heaven is opened, and the gates of hell disclosed. It is the traveler's map, the pilgrim's staff, the pilot's compass, the soldier's sword, and the Christian charter.

2. The Bible is the power of God unto eternal salvation and the source of present help for the body, soul, and spirit (Rom. 1:16, John 15:7). Christ is its grand subject, man's good, its design, and the glory of God its end. It is a mine of wealth, the source of health, and a world of pleasure.

3. The Bible is God's will or testament to men in all ages, revealing the plan of God for man here and now and in the next life. It will be opened at the judgment, and it will last forever. It involves the highest responsibility, it will reward for the least to the greatest of labor, and it will condemn all who trifle with its sacred contents.

4. The Bible is the record of God's dealings with man in the past, present, and future. It contains His message of eternal salvation for all who believe in Christ and eternal damnation for all who rebel against the gospel.

5. As a literary composition, the Bible is the most remarkable book ever made. It is a divine library of sixty-six books, some of considerable size and others no larger than a tract. These books include various forms of literature—history, biography, poetry, proverbial sayings, hymns, letters, directions for elaborate ritualistic worship, laws, parables, riddles, allegories, prophecy, and all other forms of human expression.

6. The Bible is the only book that reveals the mind of God, the state of man, the way of salvation, the door for sinners, and the happiness of believers. Its doctrine is holy, its precepts binding, its histories true, and its decisions immutable. It contains light to direct, spiritual food to sustain, and comfort to cheer. Man should read it to be wise, believe in it to be safe, and practice it to be holy; he should read it that it might fill his memory, rule his heart, and guide his feet in righteousness and true holiness. He should read it slowly, frequently, prayerfully, meditatively, searching, devotionally and study it constantly, perseveringly, and industriously, through and through until it becomes a part of his being, generating faith that will move mountains.

   B - Basic
   I - Instruction
   B - Before
   L - Leaving
   E - Earth

God Is Good

This is a testimony of how God blessed me in the midst of a difficult work environment and blessed me with a better situation than I could have imagined. To start, I will give a little background. Since the time I was a young kid, I have always loved computers and electronics. In my family, growing up, I became the go-to tech person whenever anyone had questions about technology or a problem with their computer. So naturally, I ended up going to college and getting a degree in computer technology.

After graduating college, I gravitated toward the specific field of educational technology (also known as EDTECH) for my working career. I have worked at different universities and other environments with a focus on learning technologies. Overall, I've had good experiences in my working career. However, one job, in particular, was challenging to both my career and my faith in God.

When I initially started working for this company, I had a good experience getting acclimated and learning my new role. However, as time went on, I began to face challenges with my team members as well as with the leadership. I began to feel isolated and not a part of the team. Though I was successful in completing my work tasks, I began to notice small things that were said and done to me only, but not to the others on my team. Throughout that time, I did my best to keep a positive attitude and continue fulfilling my job responsibilities. However, this job started to affect my relationship with my family and with God. I would often come home with a sad and downcast demeanor.

I would begin to question why God would allow me to be in such a working environment, and why He wasn't causing things to change for the better. What I did not realize at the time was that God had me there for a reason. I believe that He wanted me to grow as a man and as a child of God. I believe that He wanted me to learn to still have an attitude of love toward others through the course of this difficult time. I believe that He wanted me to learn to put my faith only in Him and not rely on others for approval or affirmation.

As time went on, I continued to experience the same things but began to learn how to approach these situations differently. As I learned to lean more on Christ, I began to deal better internally when these situations arose. I even began to see some of my relationships with others on the job improve.

Eventually, I would come across a posting for a job with a different company but still in the EDTECH field. Though I did not qualify fully for this role, I was excited at possibly working for this company, and I agreed with the values that it stood for. Overall, I thought it would be a great career move for me. I decided to apply for the position and prayed for God's will regardless of the outcome. Shortly after, I received a phone call from this company for an initial follow up, then a few weeks later was scheduled for an in-person interview. The interview went great, and

I was hopeful about the position. A short time later, I received a call with an offer for the new position! My first reactions were much excitement and thankfulness to God that He would allow me the opportunity to work there.

After starting this new role, I had a conversation with the leadership, and it was mentioned that they waited over a year to fill this position. They interviewed many candidates that were more qualified than me and with the work experience but did not have the unique personality and demeanor that I had. They said that they were looking for someone with a good mix of my skill set and my personality and that it took over a year to find me! When I heard this, I immediately thought back to my time at my previous job. It was all about perfect timing. God was keeping me there to grow and mature me while, at the same time, preparing this new position for me. In the end, it all worked out with his perfect timing.

After being in this new position for some time now, I am happy to report that it has truly been a blessing. God knew what He was doing. I am in a work environment that is affirming of my skills and abilities while also being challenging, and one with many growth opportunities. I work in a team environment where everyone is mutually respectful of each other, and we all want the best outcomes for the team. I can truly say that this is the best job that I have had in my career thus far.

To close this testimony, I just want to encourage the reader to trust God in whatever situation you are in. Whether a hopeful and encouraging time or a hard and difficult circumstance, God is present and with you in all things. He may have you in that circumstance to grow you and prepare you for a greater situation than you could imagine. God is good!

Testimony of Michael Lockett, Indianapolis, Indiana

The Craftiness of God

I am a believer that God will teach and guide you every step of the way when going through rough situations in your life. I was going through a divorce and dealing with plenty of negative emotions. Feelings of loneliness and depression were constantly weighing me down. I was left raising three children of my own. Two of my children were toddlers, and the youngest was an infant. During that crisis, I was incredibly young.

My oldest sibling was pregnant and had asked if I was interested in crocheting a blanket for her baby. She believed that, by me crocheting the blanket, it would help ease the pain and discomfort that I was enduring. I quickly declined from doing it. My sibling never gave up asking me to crochet the blanket. She eventually backed off for a while, giving me time to think it over. Finally, she gave me some positive advice. She felt deeply concerned about how I was constantly showing negative evidence dealing with the divorce. She told me that by crocheting the baby blanket, it might help to ease the discomfort that I was dealing with. I honestly believe God was dealing with her to share that with me. It did help to motivate and encourage my desire to give it another try.

I finally gained enough confidence believing that I could crochet the baby blanket. From past experience of crocheting, I found it to be a fun and great hobby to do. Eventually, I had slackened in my interest in crocheting because understanding the steps of each pattern had become very confusing for me. I would crochet using my own creativity in completing each project. I was not completely satisfied with that accomplishment. I desired to master and learn how to understand all the instructions in a crochet pattern.

The project that my sibling had given me to work on was organized. It had all the materials included in the kit as to how to crochet the baby blanket. There was only one issue that I was battling with pertaining to the project. I assumed that understanding the pattern instructions was going to be a huge challenge for me to handle. The problem was already being resolved because God was in control of it. I prayed and asked him to give me the knowledge on how to work through the pattern. God did just what I asked him for.

"Ask, and it shall be given you; seek, and ye shall find; knock, and it shall be opened unto you:" (Matt. 7:7–8 KJV).

I did crochet the baby blanket by understanding all the instructions for the pattern. Crocheting the blanket was a great adventurous experience for me. It had turned out to be a successful and beautiful project.

In the process of crocheting the baby blanket, it did help to ease the horrific depressed feelings from dealing with the divorce. My confidence had come back, and I began to believe that I could understand each pattern's instructions of what I chose to crochet. I had gained much crocheting experience from the previous years. It would be so challenging at times to put it to rest. That is how much I enjoy doing the work.

Now, I have desires to crochet and sell my craftwork. I have, in the past, crocheted many kinds of items. At this time now, I only specialize in crocheting bedspreads, quilts, baby blankets, child afghans, adult afghans, potholders, and coaster sets. I truly thank God for seeing me through all.

"I will instruct thee and teach thee in the way which thou shalt go: I will guide thee with mine eye" (Ps. 32:8 KJV).

God has truly been my teacher and had faithfully guided me through this journey.

Testimony of Cynthia Williams, Michigan City, Indiana

David Walls, Gary, Indiana

My God Can Do Anything

I will never forget the time when I was so sick in the hospital. When doctors gave up on my sickness since I could not be healed, God touched and healed my body. I am so thankful to be serving a miracle-working God who will say yes when doctors say no. The Lord God is a wonderful saving God. I bless his holy name. He has worked so many miracles in my life. I thank him every day. Who will not serve a God like this?

Jesus said, "And in that day ye shall ask me nothing. Verily, Verily, I say unto you, Whatsoever ye shall ask the Father in my name, he will give it you" (John 16:23 KJV). So glad I said yes to the Lord, and he saved and healed me. I know the Lord Jesus is a healer. "If ye shall ask any thing in my name, I will do it" (John 14:14 KJV). Praise his wonderful name. God will work a miracle for anyone who will believe and obey his word.

Jesus said, "Behold, I stand at the door, and knock: If any man hears my voice, and open the door, I will come in to him, and will sup with him, and he with me"(Rev. 3:20 KJV). He is knocking at the door of someone's heart today! Say yes to Jesus and be saved.

Now at the age of ninety-six years, I am still serving this wonderful God and will serve him to the end. A servant in God's will.

Testimony of Geneva Lockett, Merrillville, Indiana

God Spared My Life

God is good! God is merciful! God spared my life eighteen years ago when I was about to have prostate cancer spreading throughout my body. It all started when I was at work in my office, and my wife, Arletta, called me on the telephone. She had reminded me several days earlier about taking my physical examination, and the telephone call that day was another reminder. As I had done in the past, I informed her that I would make a doctor's appointment when I have the time to do that. Moreover, I told her I feel exceptionally good with my body. However, my wife, being the loving and caring person that she is, made the doctor's appointment for me without my knowledge. She had never done that before. My first reaction was to cancel the appointment and reschedule it for a more convenient time on my work schedule. But then, she told me that God had spoken to her and told her to make the appointment for me. Of course, at that time, I decided to keep the appointment.

I went to the doctor's appointment and included with my physical examination was a PSA test regarding the condition of my prostate. The doctor advised me that the test result was a little elevated. He then scheduled me for a biopsy. Arletta and I were concerned about the need for me to take a biopsy. The biopsy was painful for me to take, and Arletta was with me in the room. Although I was given a pill for the pain, I still felt some pain. Arletta later told me that it was difficult for her to watch me go through the pain.

The next day, I got a call from the doctor with the bad news that I had prostate cancer. The biopsy Gleason score is on a scale of 1–10, and my score was 6. The doctor advised me that a Gleason score of 7 or above could be fatal, meaning that the cancer could have spread, and surgery would not be helpful. Furthermore, the doctor told me that if I had waited any longer for the PSA test and biopsy, the cancer most likely would have spread throughout my body. I had the surgery eighteen years ago and had the cancer cells removed from my prostate.

Prostate cancer is sometimes called a silent killer because men could have prostate cancer with no warning symptoms as it was in my situation. I am a witness that our God is merciful. I thank the almighty God for sparing my life and speaking to my wife.

Testimony of Jeremiah Lockett Sr., Indianapolis, Indiana

God Kept Me

God has been so good to me down through the years. God kept me when I was possessed with an evil spirit. During a church meeting, I hit the glass window in the door at the church I was visiting. My arm was cut badly. I could have bled to death. I got thirty-three stitches in my arm.

God was watching over me once again when I was running away from home in Gary, Indiana, and walked the highway to Chicago, Illinois. I thank God for His love and protection.

"The angel of the LORD encampeth round about them that fear him, and delivereth them" (Ps. 34:7 KJV).

I had two nodules in my throat and my appendix removed as well. God took me through both surgeries. I thank God for all he has done for me in my life and my walk with Him as a child of God. God has answered all my prayers.

"But the God of all grace, who hath called us unto his eternal glory by Christ Jesus, after that ye have suffered a while, make you perfect, stablish, strengthen, settle you. To him be glory and dominion for ever and ever. Amen" (1 Pet. 5: 10–11 KJV).

Testimony of David Walls, Gary, Indiana

Encouraging Thoughts

Life is God's gift to you. The way you live your life is your gift to God. Make it a fantastic one.

—Leo Buscaglia

The beauty of the earth, the beauty of the sky, the order of the stars, the sun, the moon...their very loveliness is their confession of God.

—Augustine

Scatter seeds of kindness everywhere you go; Scatter bits of courtesy— watch them grow and grow. Gather buds of friendship; keep them till full-blown; you will find more happiness than you have ever known.

—Amy R. Raabe

Timothy Andrew Lockett, Columbus, Ohio

I Thank God

God has brought me through a lot from living in Chicago, Illinois, to Gary, Indiana. I thank God for all He has done for me. About two years ago, I had surgery to remove two large tumors from my stomach. They had grown over a period of eight years in my body. God truly blessed me while going through the surgery. Although I was in the hospital for a week, God blessed me by having health insurance to cover all my medical expenses. To God be the glory for the things He has done for me.

It has been three years this July 17, 2020, since my surgery, and I am still thanking and praising God for all he has done for me. I do not know where I would be without God in my life. He is my healer and everything to me. God is still blessing me every day.

"But thanks be to God, which giveth us the victory through our Lord Jesus Christ" (1 Cor. 15: 57 KJV).

Testimony of Vera Walls, Gary, Indiana

A Tribute to God

Praise the Lord and greetings in the precious name of Jesus.

The goodness of the Lord overwhelms us at the writing of this letter, and I trust the same on your behalf.

Let me start from the beginning, August 11, 1986. I then realized a serious ailment in my body. The symptoms were fever, weakness, loss of weight, and constant pain in the lower abdomen. Upon going to the doctor's office, he later realized the need to have me admitted to the hospital. On August 23, I entered the Broadway Methodist hospital in Merrillville, Indiana, and remained there until August 30, undergoing a series of X-rays and internal tests. They were not able to diagnose the reason behind my experience of constant pain in the lower abdomen. I continued to suffer the pain, and at times, they seemed unbearable. I was informed by my brother of a urologist, who is one who specializes in prostate and lower organs. I contacted the specialist office and received an appointment, went to visit him. And upon an examination, he diagnosed my condition to be a serious prostate infection and suggested that I reenter the hospital for further treatments. On the sixteenth day of the month of September 1986, I reentered the St. Catherine Hospital in East Chicago, Indiana, and underwent further treatments, but none of the treatments bettered my condition. My doctor, the urologist specialist, he seemed to become weary because of my lack of response to the treatments. He did not want to perform surgery because of the serious nature of the infection, and I was becoming weary, discouraged, and very depressed. And my depression increased to the point where I had given up. The pain, the weakness, and nothing they did helped my situation. But thanks be to God, who is concerned and proves his concern for his people.

I did not know that my daughter and my wife were working to get help for me. My daughter, Sister Arletta Lockett, who resides in the city of Indianapolis, knew about God's servant, Evangelist Mildred Boyd, and she made several phone calls to get in contact with her, and finally, she did. Sister Boyd was on the East Coast in the state of Massachusetts. Then she finally got in touch with her, and she told Sister Boyd of the need, which was an emergency, because I was extremely sick, even to the point of dying. But on the twenty-fifth day of September 1986, when my sweet wife visited the hospital room on that day, she told me Evangelist Mildred Boyd was going to call the hospital. All this was good news. I was eagerly waiting for the phone to ring. That same afternoon, at about two thirty-five, the phone in the hospital room rang. Sister Walls answered the phone, and Sister Boyd was on the other end, about 1,600 miles away. She had Sister Walls put me on the phone. I greeted her in the name of the Lord Jesus and assured her who I was. Evangelist Boyd prayed the prayer of faith over the phone, and immediately after hanging up the phone, I got up from a sickbed after being confined seven days at Broadway Methodist and ten days at St. Catherine hospital and *God immediately raised me up.*

I was not ashamed to praise God for His healing power. I got up from a sick bed, put my housecoat on, and went down the hall, praising God for his healing power. The nurses knew it, and those that were working on the floor knew it because I was not ashamed to praise God. On the morning of September 26, I was released from the hospital, healed. Thank God for servants like Evangelist Mildred Boyd.

Testimony of the Late District Elder, Ernest Walls Sr., Gary, Indiana

There Is Nothing That I Cherish More

When in darkness, you give light
When I am blind, you give sight
When I am down, you lift me up
With a comfort that shines so bright
If I fall, you pick me up and tell me to try again
For you gave me the power to win
It is you, God, that my life is for
And there is nothing that I cherish more.

Timothy Andrew Lockett, Columbus, Ohio

God Did It Again

My testimony started with church service three years ago. I was ushering and praising God when I discovered I could no longer see the vision board in front of the church. I had no symptoms, just lost vision in my left eye. I went home, and the next day, when passing the mirror, that was when I discovered my pupil was larger than my right eye. I called my eye doctor's office; it was a holiday, so I said I will go to the emergency room. They gave me a specialist to call. I called, and they told me to come in still. There were no symptoms; the technician checked the pressure on my eye and rechecked it. She left the office and brought the doctor back, and they kept checking my pressure. The doctor started asking me questions, did I have a headache? was I nauseated and passing out? My answer was no to everything. He was scratching his head and said I had to have some symptoms. I told him I was in church, praising God, and all of a sudden, I could not see the vision board in the front of the church. The doctor said he was going to have to do some surgery on me now. They gave me a pill and told me to sit in the waiting room. I was clueless. I did not know what was happening. I called my pastor, and he prayed for me over the phone. They called me back for my surgery and told me my eye pressure was up, and they had to bring it down. The technician asked if they needed to get me to Nashville. It was rush hour then. His reply was no. The doctor did laser surgery in his office with a thick magnifying glass and the laser. I counted the pings, about thirty-five. He stopped because he said my eye was bleeding. He asked me to go to his Nashville office in the morning; it was larger and better equipped. They gave me some eye drops to use that night.

Twenty-five years ago, I was diagnosed with narrow angle glaucoma. I was instructed to come to the emergency room if I had symptoms. I never experienced any symptoms. God was good to me. I prayed for my healing. They continued the laser surgery in the morning, another twenty-five more pings. Later, I found out my eye pressure was seventy-one. I asked if anyone lost their vision. They said yes; a lady had just lost her vision. God healed and blessed me.

"And he cometh to Bethsaida; and they bring a blind man unto him, and besought him to touch him. And he took the blind man by the hand, and led him out of the town; and when he had spit on his eyes, and put his hands upon him, he asked him if he saw ought" (Mark 8:22–23 KJV).

God blessed me after being out of the navy for forty-one years. I found out I was blessed with benefits due to a sergeant doing his job. I had an eye examination for glasses; my doctor said I needed a cataract removed ASAP. I went to the VA; they told me I was complicated like every eye doctor. My problem is that there is not enough space in my eye orbit where instruments could reach into. I was scheduled for the removal of a cataract. The doctor said it would take two hours to three and a half hours. My lens was replaced with what they had on hand. I needed a different lens. My vision did not improve, so I needed another eye surgery. The doctor said there was nothing to hold my lens in place; my iris was attached to my cornea. He had to suture the lens to hold it in place. The VA sent me to a specialist after several months of testing my vision. I could only see the big E during an eye test. I asked God to heal my eyes and bless me with a good surgeon. I never lost faith. I believed God from the beginning for my healing. God has never let me down. "Even so faith, if it hath not works, is dead, being alone" (Ja. 2:17) (Ja 2: 18–20 KJV). I have now had my second eye surgery, the second lens replaced after several months, and the sutures removed from my cornea. My eyesight is much better. I can read the third and fourth lines on the eye chart. God has allowed me to see to continue his work of being a servant.

Testimony of Rachael Dotson, Smyrna, Tennessee

To God Be the Glory

My name is Sheryl. I didn't always know the Lord like I do now, and I'm so thankful that God saved me and loved me when I wasn't loveable. I was raised Catholic, and the love for Christ just wasn't the love that I have now, which is as a personal savior. It was God that opened my eyes and came into my heart.

My husband (Ralph) and I met at Fort Knox, Kentucky, which was also the place where we got married. From Kentucky, the army sent us to Fort Wainwright, Alaska, and then to Fort Stewart, Georgia. We lived off base in Hinesville, which is where we purchased our home, and that's where God intertwined with me, and my life and my family's life changed for good. Base housing was hard to find, and the waiting list was very long.

God was working, we found our home. A lot of people within the neighborhood were in the service as well. But the Lord put us next to the right one, a Christian family. Oh, how very important it is to invite people to church. Our neighbor invited me and my family to church, and I said, "Yes, I would love to go." Ralph was away at the time. He worked very hard and was away a lot and had to do a lot of training.

God blessed us with two children, John and Joshua, two wonderful boys. It was on a Sunday when we walked into the church and was greeted by a man I called Brother Bill. Everyone in this church was so friendly and kind. You could feel the warmth and friendliness, which made you feel welcome. I could never forget how much happiness and joy was in this Holiness church. There was something surely different; now I know, but I didn't at the time. It was the presence of the Lord. The music was beautiful, and the entire service was so special.

We kept going, and when my husband came back, I was telling him about church and service, so the next Sunday, he went with me and the children. He liked the church, service, and the people. But the army kept him busy and sending him away.

God was dealing with me though in his own tender, loving way. I wanted to have the joy and happiness I witnessed as others were having. I begin going to the altar, praying, not knowing for sure what or how I needed to pray because of my upbringing. But I knew that I needed to be saved. How great is our God that we just come as we are and ask for forgiveness? Praise the Lord. His mercy endures forever.

Glory be to God. One Sunday, I went to the altar, and God saved me, and not just me but my son, John, who was about nine years old at the time. Josh was three at the time. When Joshua was a little older, the Lord saved him too. Ralph gave his heart to the Lord and was saved.

I continued going to the altar and praying, and I was baptized with the sweet Holy Ghost.

Throughout our forty years, we have had our ups and downs, but God has prevailed and seen us through. He has always been so good and faithful. God never fails; He is always on time. God says, "Be strong and of a good courage, fear not, nor be afraid of them: for the Lord thy God, he it is that doth go with thee; he will not fail thee, nor forsake thee" (Deut. 31:6 KJV).

Testimony of Sheryl A. Julian, Troy, Ohio

Faith

Four years ago, God gave me a vision to have another daughter and to name her Faith. Little did I know that that vision was something that God would use to work in my life to grow my faith. I had to have faith, trusting in God's promise to me when we ran into challenges when trying to conceive. Eventually, we came to the understanding that conception was on God's timetable, not ours. After a year and a half of waiting for God, we found out we were expecting. We were overly excited. However, early in the pregnancy, we found out that there was a complication. This was another opportunity for us to trust God and walk with faith. Early in the second trimester, the doctor planned for a scheduled cesarean at thirty-five–thirty-six weeks. Unfortunately, I went into labor at twenty-eight weeks, which put us in a life-threatening situation. Little did we know, God was going to perform a miracle in our lives. God provided everything that we needed that night to keep us alive.

Faith spent three months in the NICU. Although those were some tough times, we knew God was with us because we had great support from family, friends, and our church. We were filled with so much joy the day Faith came home. There are times we look at her in awe of God. "Let us hold fast the profession of our faith without wavering; for he is faithful that promised;" (Heb. 10:23 KJV). Let us hold tightly without wavering to the hope we affirm, for God can be trusted to keep His promise. I pray that you will experience who God is and that you will know Him to be who He says He is.

Testimony of Michelle M. Lockett, Troy, Ohio

The Pressing

Oh! the cares of this world and the issues of life! Down here, depression is trending and anxiety is a dominant force. So many people are stuck between meditation and medication. The pharmacy lines are constantly increasing and the doctors can't seem to write the prescriptions fast enough.

I'm not surprised the least bit because this is one depressing place. The Bible tells us that the world is passing away. "And the world passeth away, and the lust thereof: but he that doeth the will of God abideth for ever" (1 John 2:17 KJV). So we're all just basically flowing through a wilderness that is literally dying more each day until its appointed end. So many of us resemble the walking dead with our heads bowed and minds buried inside a screen that we don't even notice the enormously loud, ticking sound.

My experience and relatability grant me a first-class ticket straight to the underlying source. I know how to wear a smile better than a custom-made ball gown, but my heart hasn't danced in a while. It took me quite some time to embrace the fact that I have battled with depression and anxiety ever since I was a child. I don't resent the circumstances because God is transforming me into a warrior that can train others on how to conquer their monsters. I also don't regret having an enlarged heart and a painfully sensitive soul. I just need to keep building my indestructible fortress around the two.

On many occasions, my sweet spirit was punched open and drained until all that was left was a bitter aftertaste. Extreme heat, soar brokenness, and oxygen-snatching limitations turned me into an internal pressure cooker. Through it all, God has shielded me from developing frown implants, dehydrated pupils, and a cactus-like personality. I still desire to remain a cheerful giver because I understand that bitterness is a real silent killer.

Solomon was spot on about the wisdom and grief parallel: "For in much wisdom is much grief: and he that increaseth knowledge increaseth sorrow" (Eccl. 1:18 KJV). I know a lot, but I also hurt a lot. As an unashamed college dropout, I consider myself to be on the dean's list of life. I am pressing toward God's stage to accept my award. My steps are sometimes slow and heavy like I am wearing cement for shoes. I am also wearing a glow that this world didn't give me or can take away.

I remain ready and equipped to encourage anyone at any time because my testimony stays with me wherever I go. I am an overcomer by the words of my testimony. I thank God for turning my pain into therapy for someone else. I thank God for his keeping powers. My soul shall find rest. My words shall destroy yokes. My gifts shall make room for me. I'm still here. I'm still growing. I still have a lot to look forward to. I still trust and believe in God's plans for my life.

Testimony of Janette Williams, Michigan City, Indiana

I Am Grateful

I am grateful to have the opportunity to be a witness to the goodness of God.

God is profoundly good all the time. I am rapidly approaching three score and ten years and have experienced the good, turbulent, and heartbreaking periods that life has presented, and I can truthfully say that, through it all, God is good.

God is holy, almighty, omniscient, omnipresent, and omnipotent! He is my savior and knows the beginning and the end of every situation in my life's journey. I know God as a healer when the doctors cannot make a proper diagnosis. He is a protector, shielding me from dangers, seen and unseen. It is a blessing to know His word is true and everlasting to those who believe in Him.

God is loving and merciful, even when I do not deserve it. He loves each of us and desires that we serve and honor Him in all our ways. He will not forsake His children but will lead and guide us to do His will. It is an individual decision to obey His word. In my life's journey, I make it a routine to give thanks and praise to God in the good times as well as in the tough times, in sickness and good health, in poverty or abundance, in grief, or in success. He always deserves the praise and honor.

In conclusion, I found there is a blessing in giving God a tenth or more of your earnings, for He has blessed you with the strength and wisdom to earn. I know, from personal experience, He will multiply what you have left in so many ways, creating blessings in all areas of your life. I encourage everyone to know God for yourself and to hold fast to His everlasting word.

Testimony of Geneva Walls-Nelson, Gary, Indiana

The Battle

The piercing rays of the morning sun ascend me from slumber.

Scarred from the battle the day before, yet steadfast is my strength.

Grateful am I to the Most High for protecting me from adversarial influences.

Contemplating today's battle, my God reassures my victory over the evil one.

Then the Holy Voice speaks, "What does not destroy me strengthens me."

The quest for peace impels me to become enrobed with the shining armor of truth.

The urge for courage excites me to become armed with the shield of undying faith.

The desire for hope inspires me to lift to the heavens the conquering sword of love.

Grace offers me all the reasons to enter the battlefield one more time,

For I know my God is with me in my darkest hour.

Like a predator, I search out my opponent with a vengeance,

Seeking justice for all the wrongs that have been committed.

Suddenly, the enemy attacks with the forces of indolence, ignorance, and idolatry. But the armor of truth defends.

Subtly, the enemy assaults with the forces of disbelief, distrust, and distress. But the shield of undying faith repels.

Finally, the enemy advances with the forces of malice, misanthropy, and misery. But the conquering sword of love renders defeat.

Standing victorious over the slain victim of evil, my eyes deceive me not. My adversary is nothing more than a reflection of the darkness that exists within. The battle conquering my darkness so my light may shine like the easter star. The sun begins to descend to its place of origin, and tranquility is king. Repose from this day's triumph, extol is my soul for God did keep.

The piercing rays of the morning sun ascends me from my slumber. Scarred from the battle the day before, yet steadfast is my strength. Grateful am I to the Most High for protecting me from adversarial influences. Contemplating today's battle, my God reassures my victory over the evil one. Then the Holy Voice speaks, "What does not destroy me strengthens me."

—Jeremiah Lockett Jr., Indianapolis, Indiana

Scriptures

"The righteousness of thy testimonies is everlasting: give me understanding, and I shall live. I cried with my whole heart; hear me, O Lord: I will keep thy statutes. I cried unto thee; save me, and I shall keep thy testimonies" (Psalm 119:144–146 KJV).

"I will bless the Lord at all times: his praise *shall* continually be in my mouth. My soul shall make her boast in the Lord: the humble shall *hear thereof,* and be glad. O magnify the Lord with me, and let us exalt his name together" (Psalm 34:1–3 KJV).

"Let them shout for joy, and be glad, that favour my righteous cause: yea, let them say continually, Let the Lord be magnified, which hath pleasure in the prosperity of his servant. And my tongue shall speak of thy righteousness and of thy praise all the day long" (Psalm 35:27–28 KJV).

"No weapon that is formed against thee shall prosper; and every tongue that shall rise against thee in judgment thou shall condemn. This is the heritage of the servants of the Lord, and their righteousness is of me, saith the Lord" (Isaiah 54: 17 KJV).

"Seek ye the Lord while he may be found, call ye upon him while he is near: Let the wicked forsake his way, and the unrighteous man his thoughts: and let him return unto the Lord, and he will have mercy upon him; and to our God, for he will abundantly pardon" (Isaiah 55:6–7).

"These things I have spoken unto you, that in me ye might have peace. In the world ye shall have tribulation: but be of good cheer; I have overcome the world" (John 16:33 KJV).

The Day I Returned to My First Love

In March 2007, I became a born-again Christian. Jesus had radically transformed my life and set me on a path different than the one I had known the previous years of my life.

But let's fast-forward to March 2019. It's the day I was baptized in the Holy Spirit. Let me explain with my personal testimony of what the Lord did for me on that beautiful day.

A friend of mine had invited me to come to hear a guest speaker at a local church in a neighboring city. The days leading up to the event, I felt so compelled to attend even though I didn't realize at the time what topic was being covered by the speaker.

As I parked and got out of my car, I went in and sat down in the front row by myself. My friend had not seen me come in. As I sat in my chair, the guest speaker started talking. I immediately realized that she was speaking about healing ministry. As soon as I realized this, I all of a sudden got really uncomfortable.

In the last twelve years of my Christian walk, in the church contexts I had been a part of, I was always taught a theology that supernatural healing didn't exist anymore. So, my red flags immediately went up, and I started to question the beliefs I had been taught thus far in my Christian walk.

As she began to speak further, I begin to have an internal dialogue with God. My inner dialogue began to wade through what I knew to be true, and at that moment, I started to question my beliefs. But doubting my beliefs and questioning felt freeing like I was exactly where I needed to be in that moment, as squeamishly as I felt, trying not to show it all on my face as to not disappoint the guest speaker. (After all, I had sat in the front row!)

My processing of this validation included the fact that I have trusted my friend who invited me, and I knew that she would not have done if the topic had been something that she didn't trust. The longer she spoke, the more I started to question my old beliefs. So, I came to a point of wrestling where I just simply didn't know what else to do except ask the Lord to give me some kind of undeniable evidence that what she was saying was trustworthy and true.

So, the previous two weeks, I had an ongoing sore throat. Every time I would swallow it would hurt *every single time*. I usually get that once a year followed by a few short days of losing my voice. So, the idea came to my mind that I could ask the Lord to heal it and see what would happen.

In the next moment, I simply asked the Lord and prayed, "Lord, if what this woman is saying is true and you want me to believe this, then would you heal my throat?"

I immediately swallowed to see if anything had happened. And the very pain I had expected might still be present *was not* there! I swallowed again. No pain! I swallowed even more again so as to look for it and in what felt like slow motion, again the pain was *not there*! The pain had been *instantly* eradicated! As I sat in that very seat. Instantly gone!

A few moments later, once I had realized what had indeed happened. I immediately started to sink down in my chair, overcome with such a feeling of love being poured out on me by God. Then the tears started coming. Long streaming tears flowed down my face. I couldn't hold back the tears. It was a cry that felt like a cleansing. It was the most powerful thing I have experienced thus far in life. Feeling and experiencing the love of God like that for the first time! Wow!

As I sat in my chair and cried, the next thing that happened struck me as if, from head to toe, I experienced the sense of a cool washing that came over my entire body. I felt different. I likened it to the same feeling I had gotten back in the spring of March 2007 when I first became a Christian, and I'm so grateful to the Lord for what he has restored in me a hungering love for Him that I so desperately didn't know I could have ever wanted or needed! Hallelujah!

In conclusion, had I not gone through that experience, I know that I would still be stiff-arming all that God has for me and my family. When I got home that day, I couldn't help sharing what had happened to me with my husband. It was the "icing on the cake" when my husband could tell that my countenance had changed and that something miraculous truly did happen to change me in an instant!

To this day, my journey in experiencing a more robust and lively relationship with the Lord stands to this day that day because of this pivotal moment in my life. I have experienced things that I didn't know were even possible on this side of heaven. It changed me, everything about me and for me. It was a returning to my first love and I'm eternally grateful!

Even though I couldn't put words to it at the time it happened, I know now that it was God's spirit washing over me, and that I was baptized in the spirit that day and that there truly is a difference between receiving the spirit at the point of salvation and receiving the baptism of the Holy Spirit.

My hope and prayer for you, reader, is peace. If my testimony is an encouragement to you, whether you identify as a Christian or not, give Jesus permission to do what only he can do. Invite Him in! That's all He needs is an invitation to do what only He can do, for He will do more than we can ask or imagine.

"Now unto him that is able to do exceeding abundantly above all that we ask or think, according to the power that worketh in us. Unto him be glory in the church by Christ Jesus throughout all ages, world without end" (Eph. 3:20–21 KJV).

Testimony of Kylie Lockett, Indianapolis, Indiana

A Day to Remember

It was a beautiful Sunday afternoon that year of 2018. I was preparing dinner for our oldest son and his family. We love having family gatherings with our children from time to time. While preparing the dinner, I did not know it would turn out to be tragic for me. I was cooking white potatoes to be mashed in my pressure cooker. I turned off the pressure cooker to let it cool down, and I would come back to it shortly. Well, I got distracted, doing other food preparations, and forgot to release the pressure off the pressure cooker before I opened it.

My pressure cooker was a tall one and sat high on the stove. When I opened the lid, the hot water and steam came out with such force; all I could do was scream. It went straight to my stomach. The force was supposed to go to my face, neck, and upper chest; instead, it went to my stomach area. When I came to the reality of what had happened, I knew right then it was God protecting me. The hot water and steam were meant for my face, but God said no! He allowed the hot water and steam to go to my stomach area. I immediately started thanking and praising God for His protective power. It was God's hands that were controlling all that hot water and steam from going up to my face. It was a miracle, and I saw it happened. I can never forget what God did for me that day.

I continued preparing the dinner in burning pain, not letting on much to my family, and we had a wonderful family gathering that evening. The next morning when I woke, I pulled up my shirt and ran to tell my husband Jerry to look! The burn was so bad, I called my sweet sister Rachael. She is a nurse, and she instructed me what to do. I went to the immediate care unit and was sent home with cream and bandages to care for the burn. It was God that protected me through it all. My face would have been disfigured for life, and my emotional well-being.

Satan knew it would have destroyed me, but God was there to protect me. I went through a long recovery period, and my sweet husband Jerry was with me every day to clean and change my wounds. Every day when I look at my stomach, I cry because it was God. He shielded and protected me. I love Him because of who He is. God is love. I know him as a healer, a protector, a provider, and in Him I have my joy and peace.

God has done so many miracles in my life journey, and this is just one testimony out of many. Thank you, Jesus, for dying for the world on the cross. I am now a child of God, and His love, grace, mercy, and protective power are in my life. Let God come into your heart and change your life. God is waiting for you with his out stretched arms to receive you.

"The angel of the Lord encampeth round about them that fear him, and delivereth them" (Psalm 34:7 KJV).

"For he shall give his angels charge over thee, to keep thee in all thy ways" (Psalm 91:11 KJV).

Testimony of Arletta Lockett, Indianapolis, Indiana

Printed in the United States
By Bookmasters